Dedication

To my parents, Pablo and artists young and old
who fill their lives with vibrancy and color.

Modern

FASHION ILLUSTRATION

40+ HIGH-FASHION GOWNS AND DRESSES TO STYLE AND COLOR

The Coloring Book

Holly Nichols, fashion illustrator and bestselling author of *Modern Fashion Illustration*

PAGE STREET
PUBLISHING CO.

PAGE STREET
PUBLISHING CO.

Published in 2024 by
Page Street Publishing Co.
27 Congress Street, Suite 1511
Salem, MA 01970
www.pagestreetpublishing.com

Distributed by Macmillan, sales in Canada by The Canadian Manda Group.

27   26   25   24   3   4   5   6

ISBN-13: 979-889-0039-927

Cover and book design by Page Street Publishing Co.
Illustrations by Holly Nichols

Printed and bound in the United States

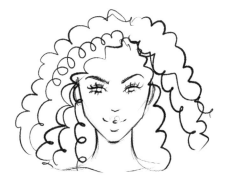 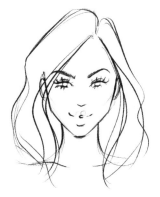 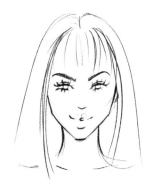

INTRODUCTION

Over the past several years, I have spoken with parents of young children, parents of grown children, former art students, current art students, young budding artists and those that left their creative passions to pursue a career. They all have the same thing in common: creating art provides them an outlet to escape the world. There is something quite relaxing about using color to create shapes and worlds—it is one of the reasons why I feel very lucky to do the work I do daily. *Modern Fashion Illustration: The Coloring Book* is a welcome into my world. I hope these coloring page recreations of the work I have enjoyed bringing to life bring you relaxation and a whimsical introduction, or reintroduction, to your imaginative potential. As an additional tool, I have included color references for each coloring page in the back of the book, which I hope serve as creative inspiration.

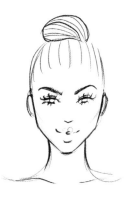 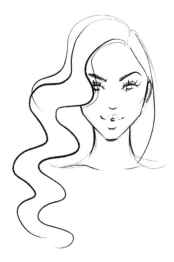 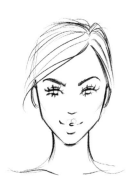

ACKNOWLEDGMENTS

Creating this coloring book has been a labor of love, and I am grateful to those who have helped and inspired me along the way.

I'd like to extend my gratitude to my family and friends for their years of cheerleading and supporting my creative endeavors. Their enthusiasm for my work continues to fuel my imagination. I'd like to thank them for often being live models and cameos in my drawing videos.

I would also like to express my appreciation for my literary agent, publishing team and all of the editors who brought this coloring book to life. Thank you for your endless hours of work and dedication to bring my ideas to fruition. Your expertise has been invaluable and provided me with great confidence.

Finally, I am deeply grateful to my followers for constantly engaging with my posts, sharing my silly videos and for tuning in daily. If even ten of you tuned in, I'd still love what I do, but having the support over 6 million makes me feel like I can do this forever.

It has been a joy to create this coloring book, and I hope it brings coloring enthusiasts, young and old, endless hours of relaxation.

ABOUT THE AUTHOR

After graduating from college with a BFA in Studio Art, Holly Nichols sought a way to merge her love of fashion with art. Her sketchbook and napkin doodles of designer duds became refined drawings. She uses her fashion-inspired illustrations to engage her extensive social media audience, sharing daily drawing videos and tutorial clips. Holly has created fashionable illustrations and artful campaigns for Saks Fifth Avenue, Barneys New York, Neiman Marcus, Disney and many more. She uses artist-quality markers to hand-sketch garments in her studio just south of Boston. Visit her website at www.hnicholsillustration.com.

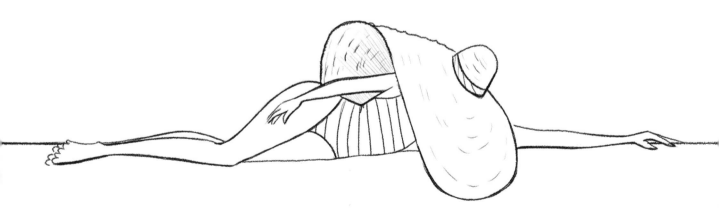

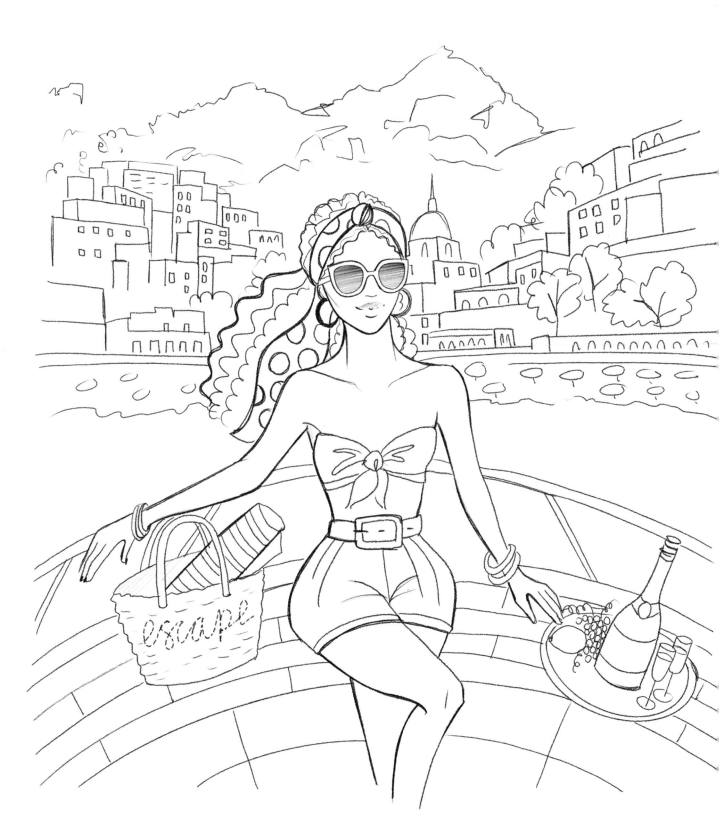

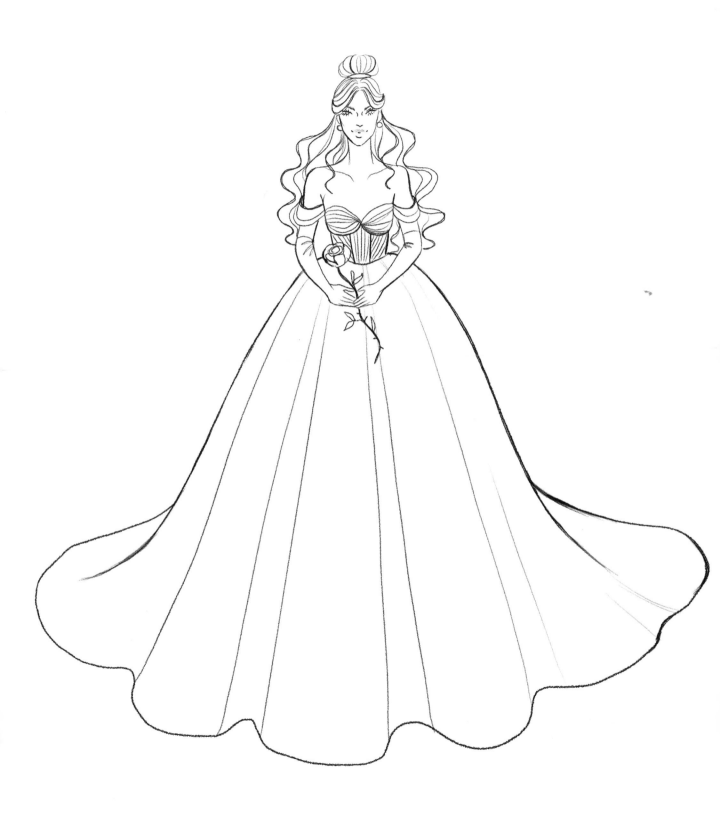

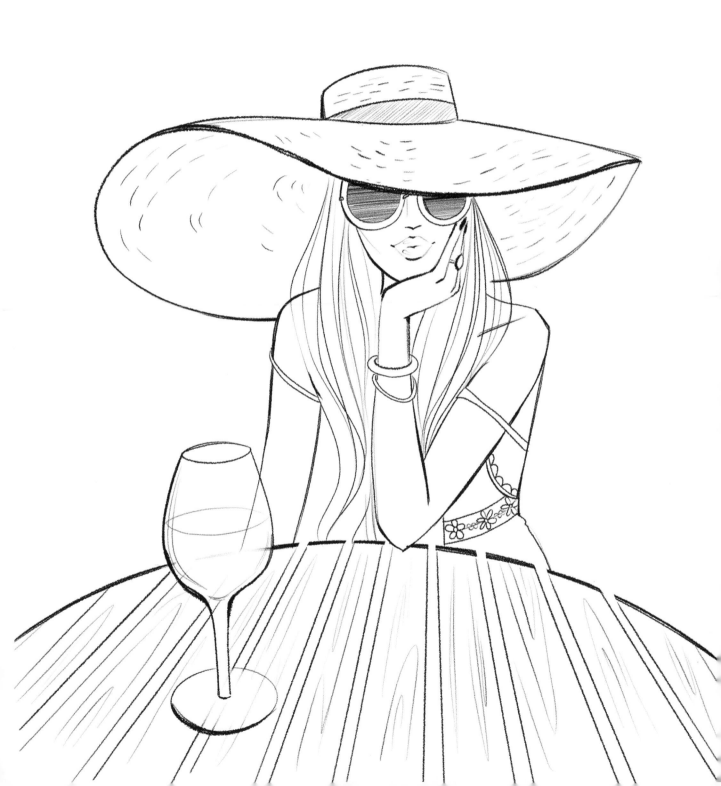

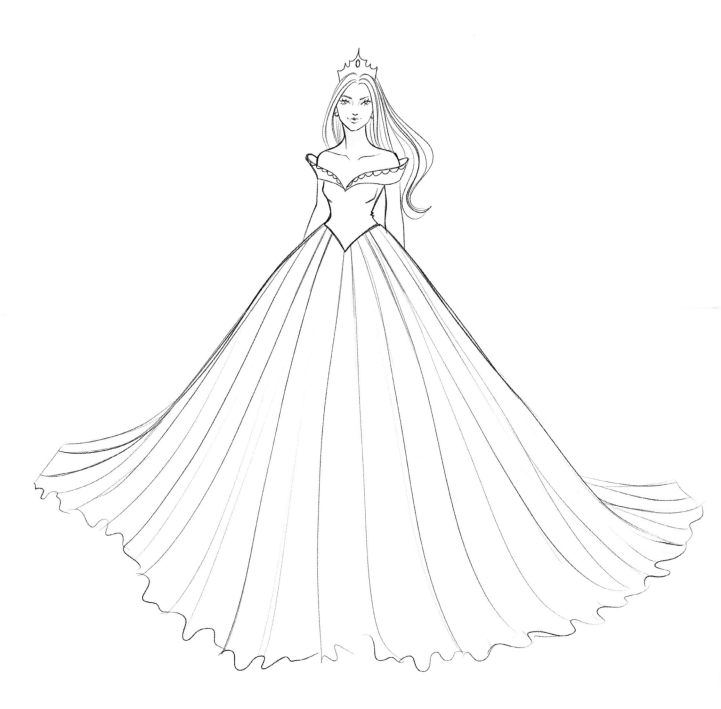

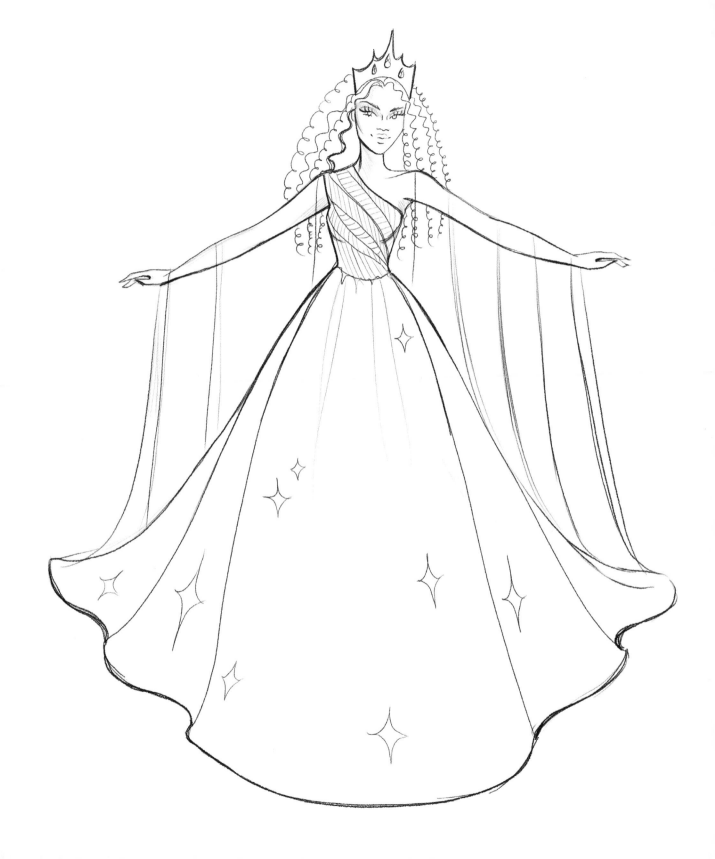

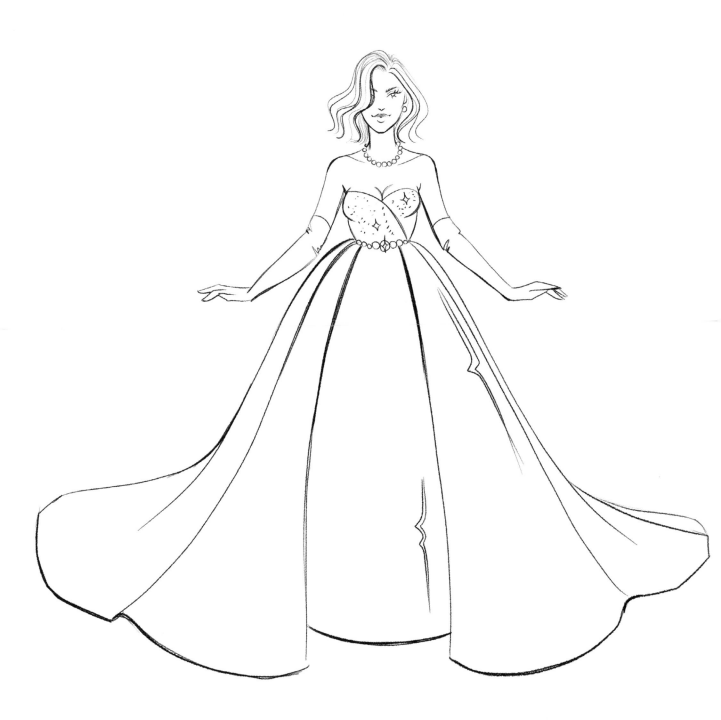

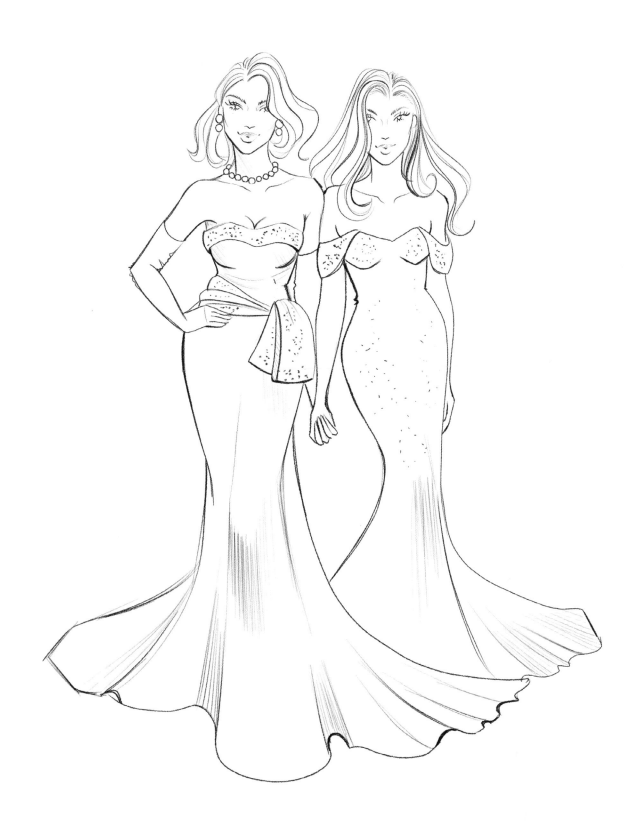

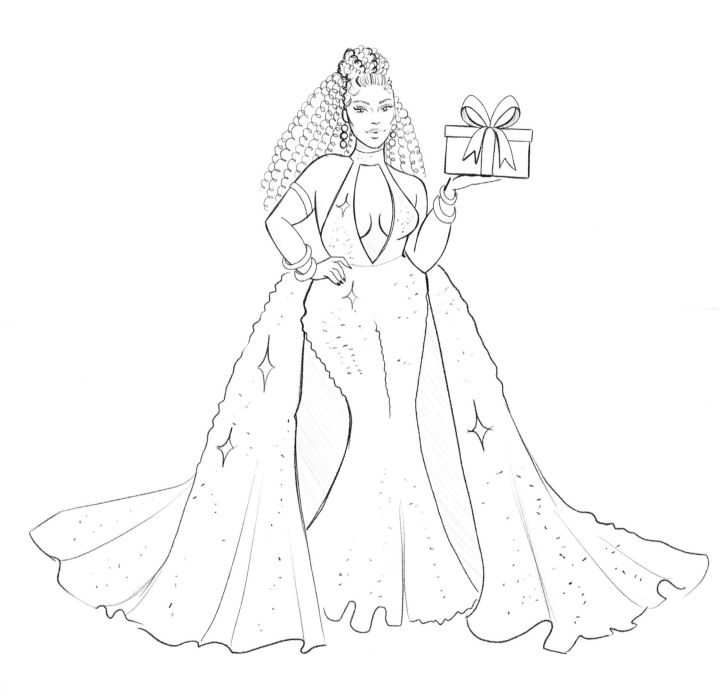

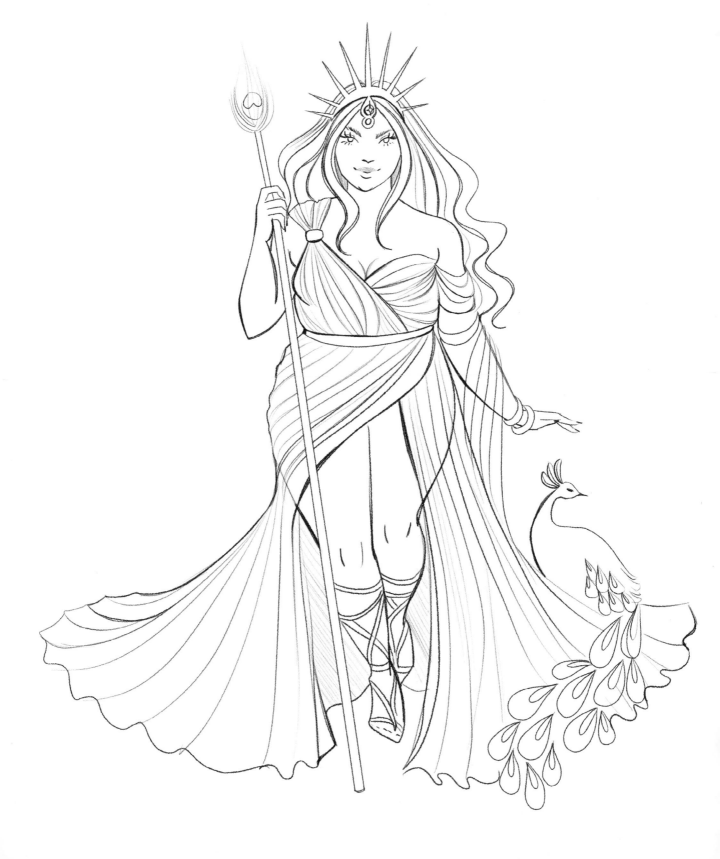

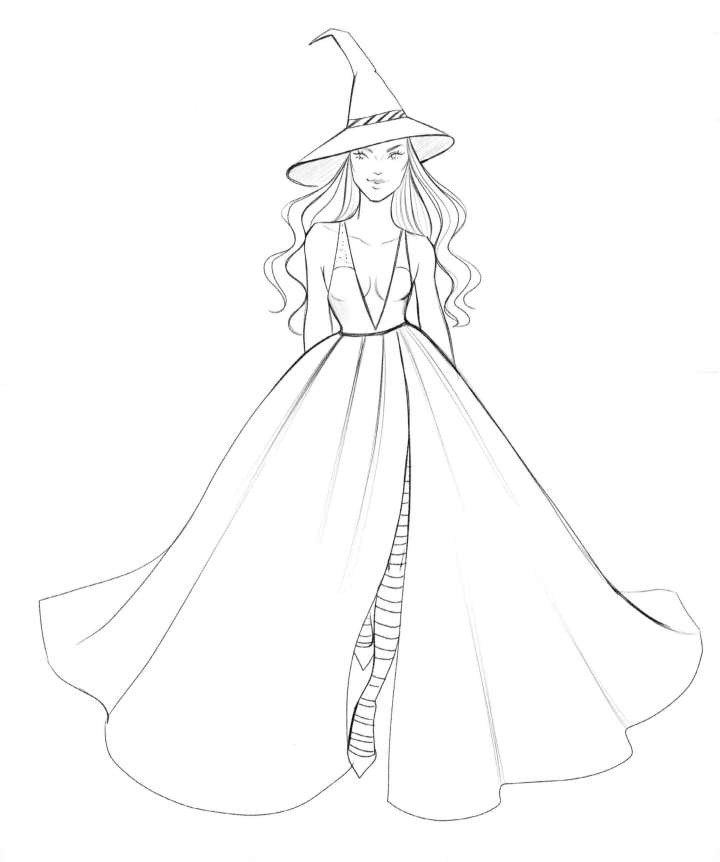

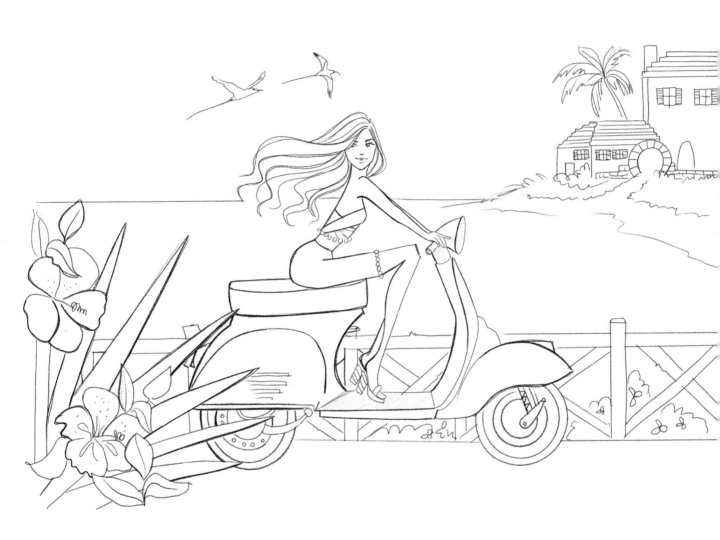

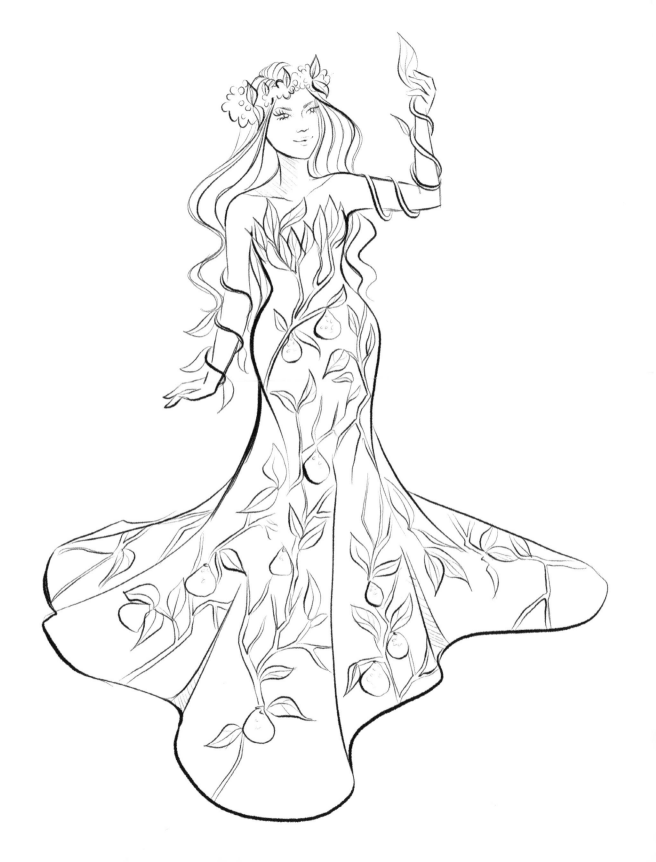

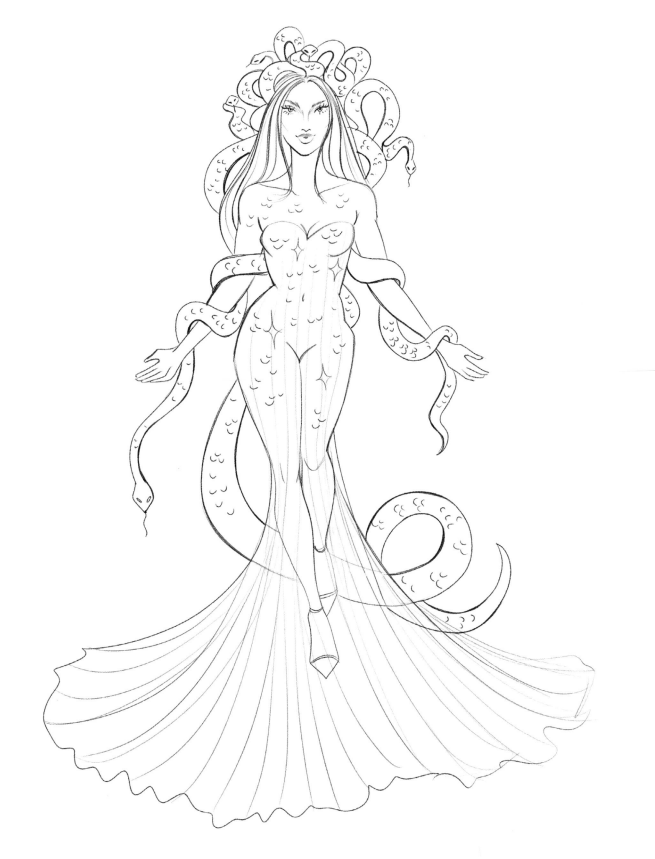

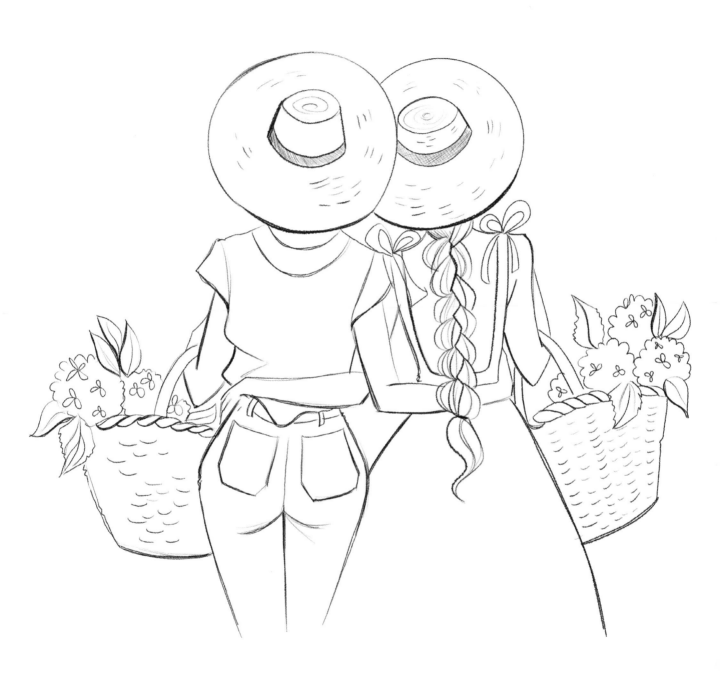

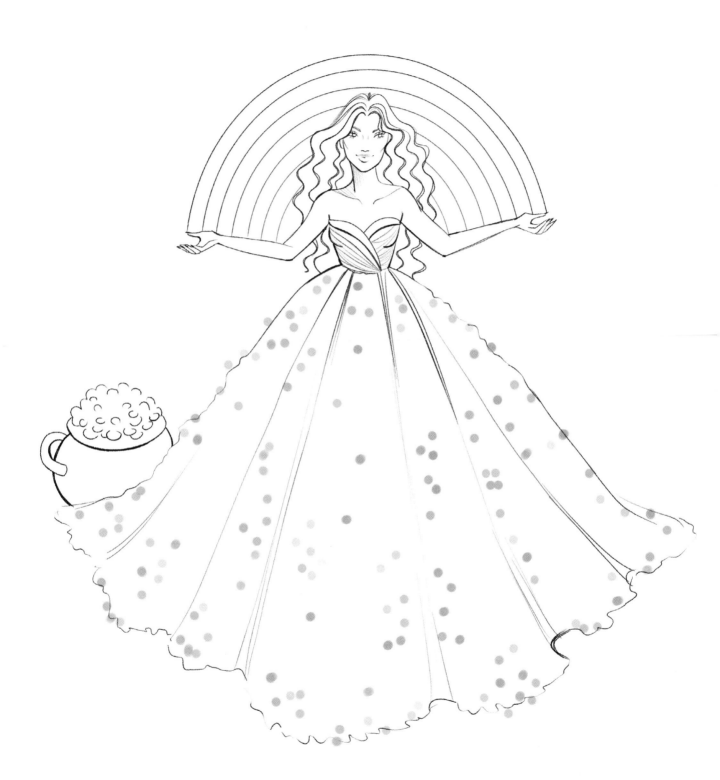

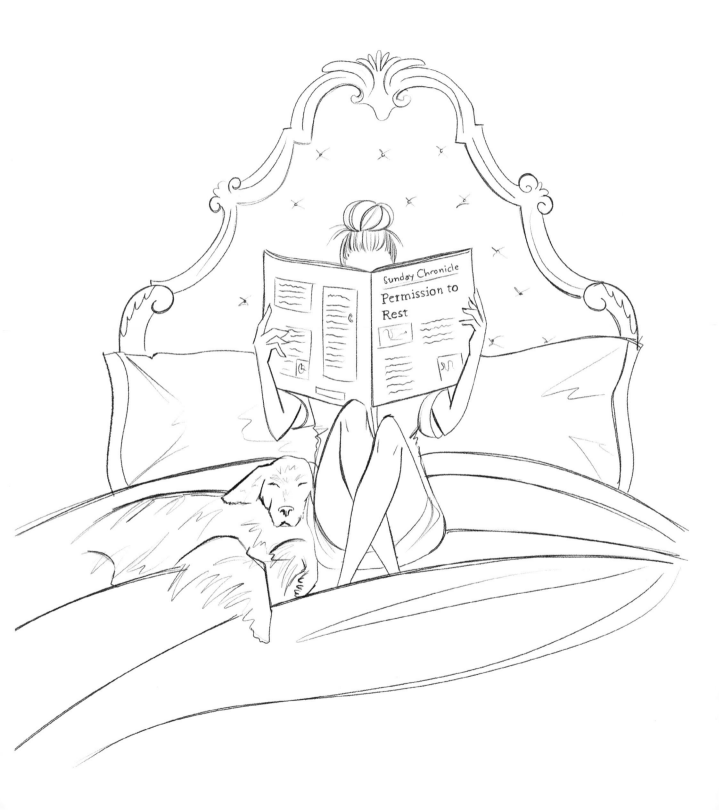

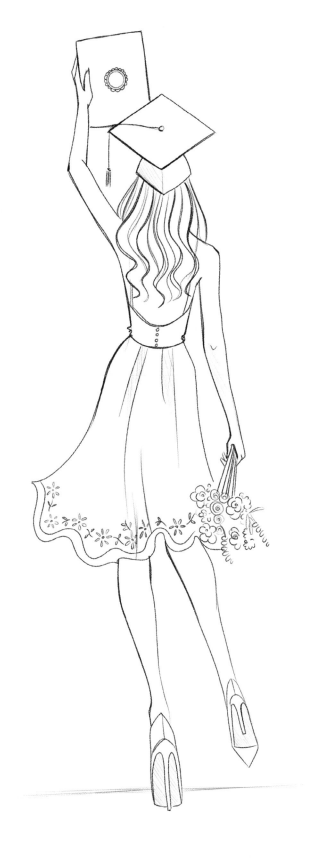

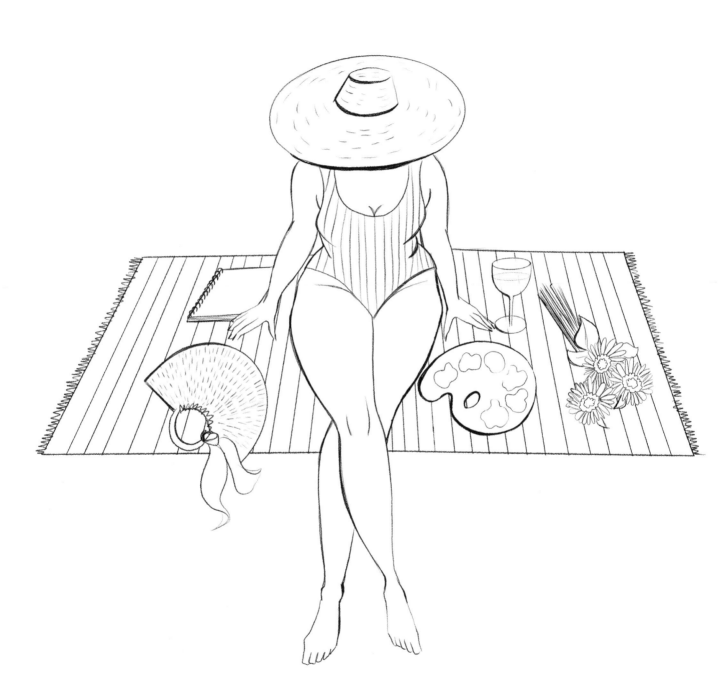

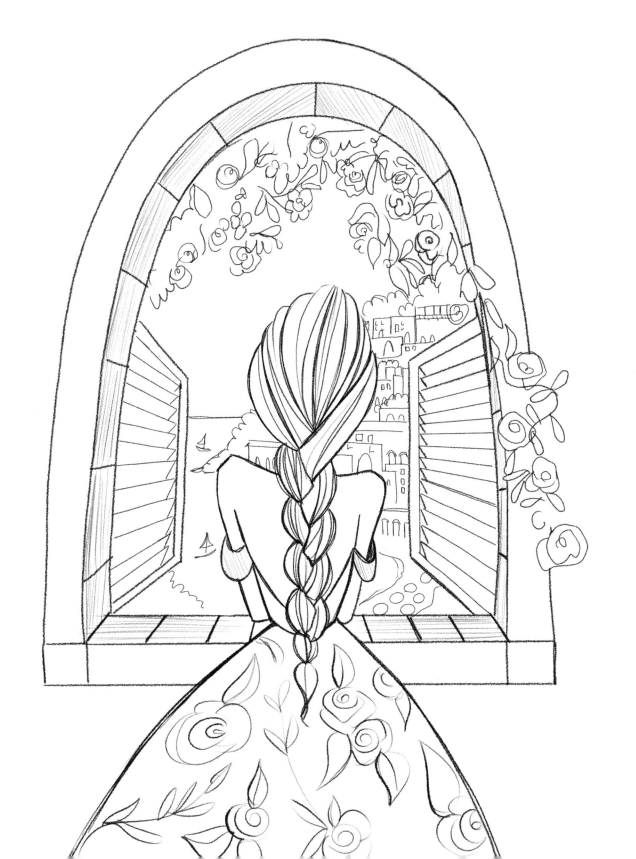

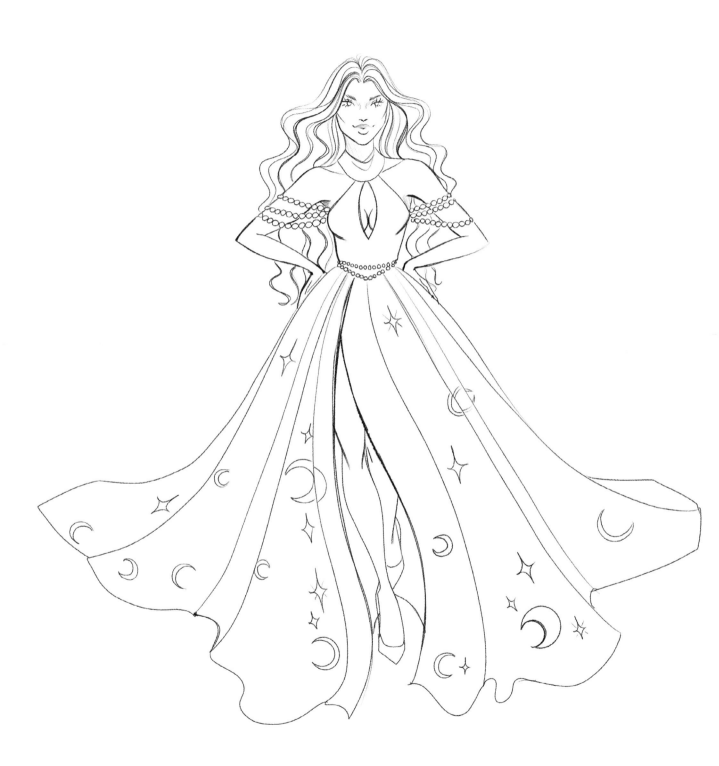

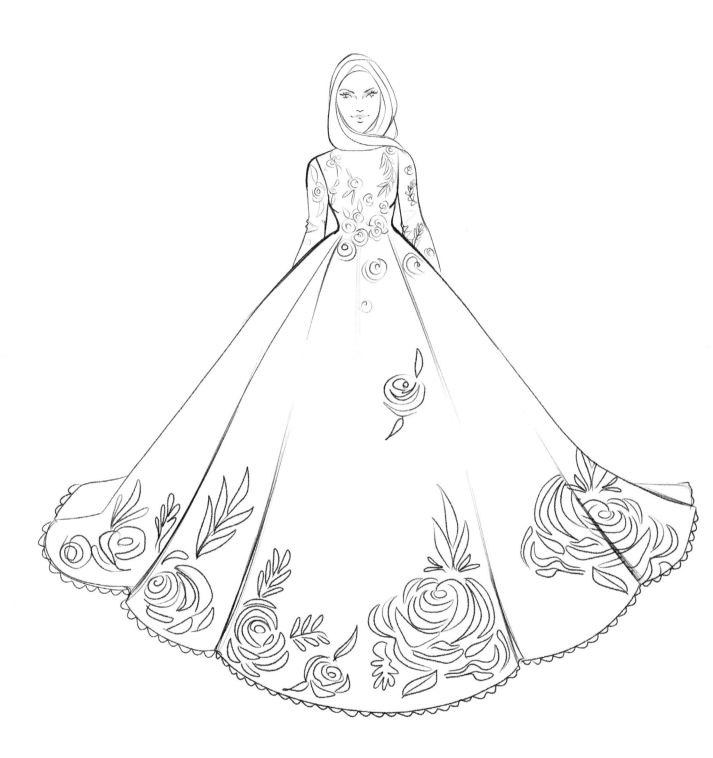

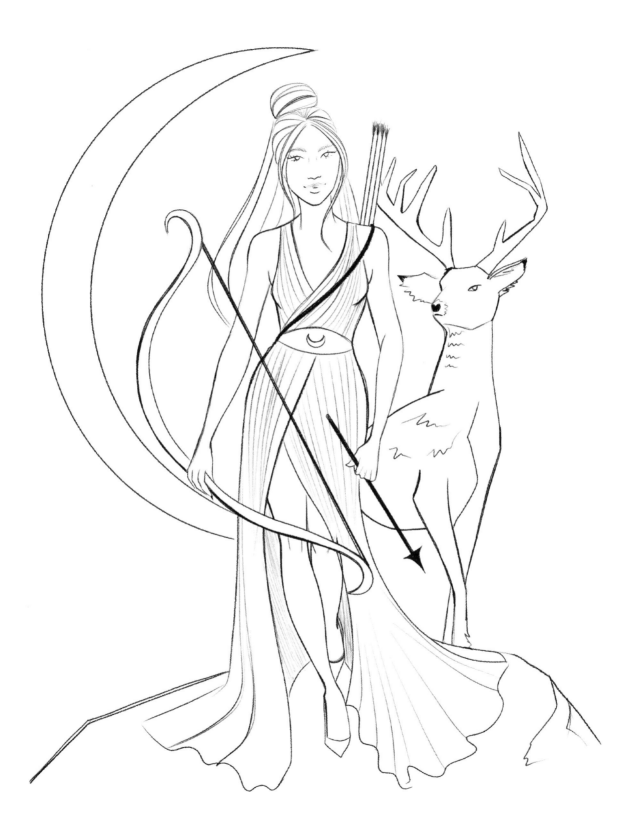

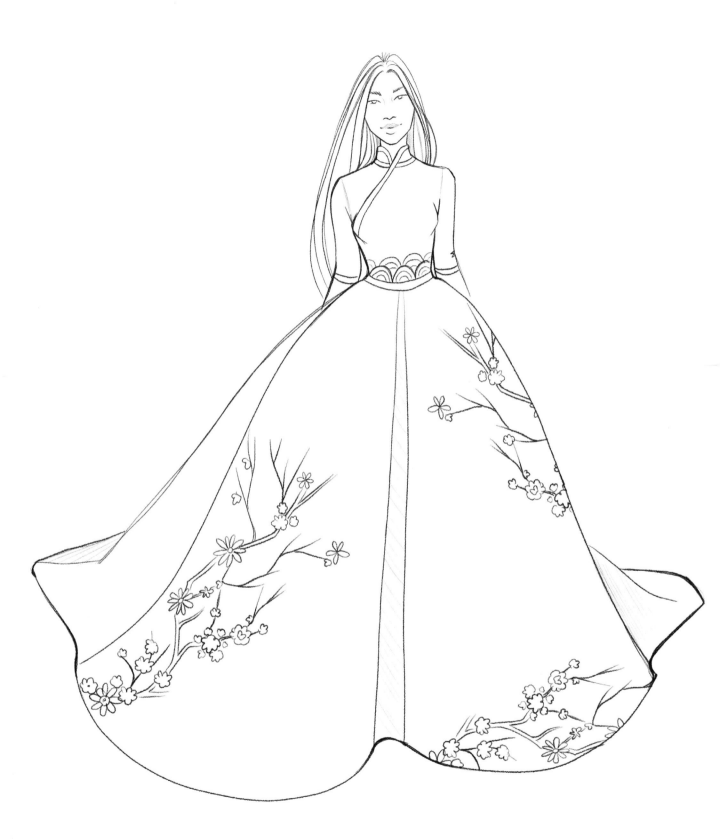

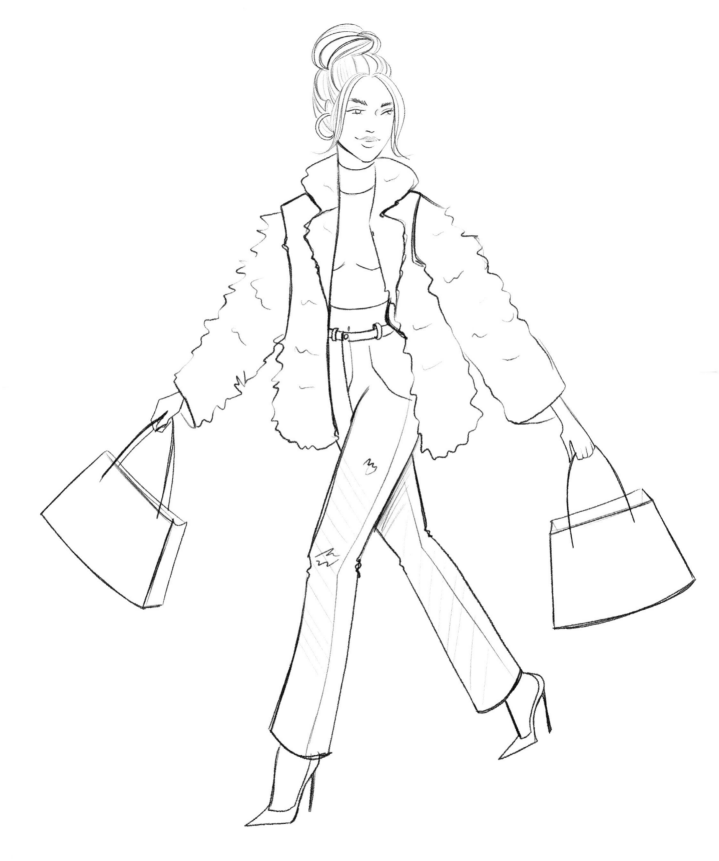

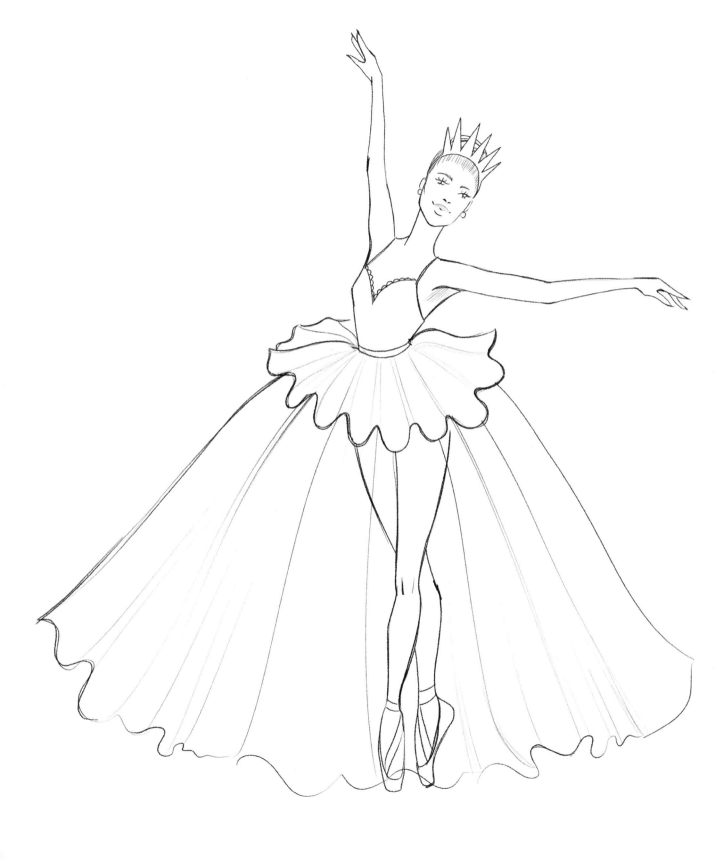

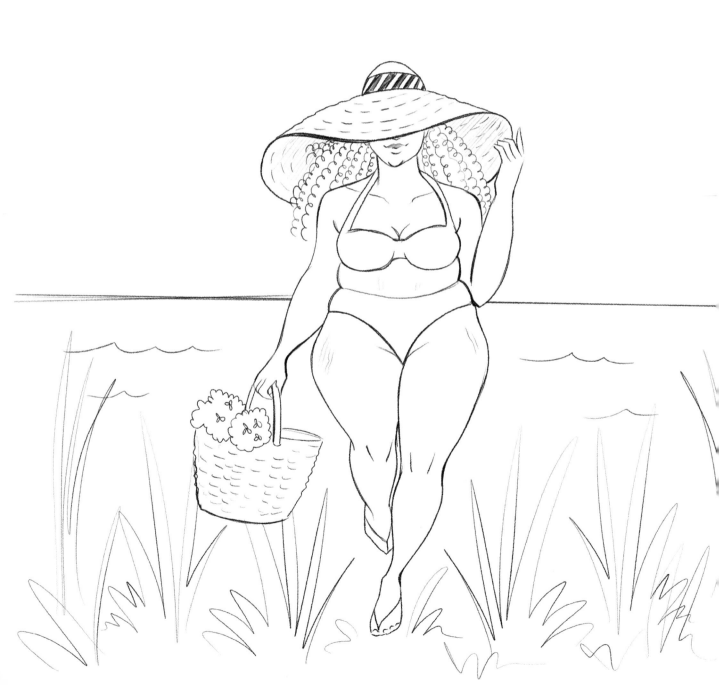

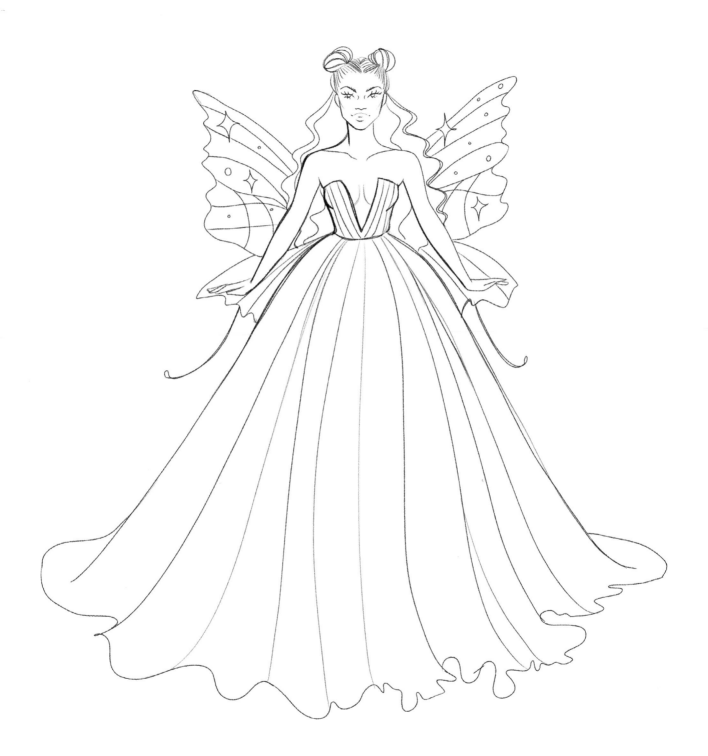

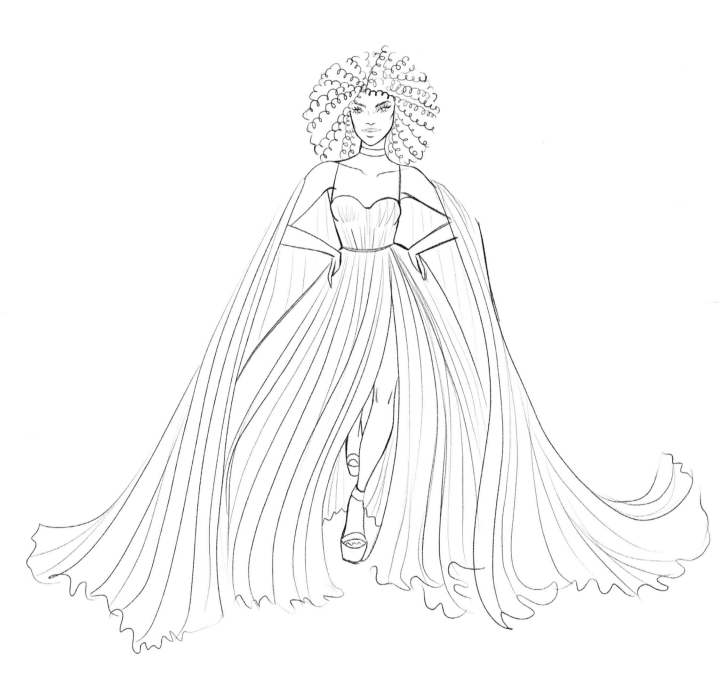

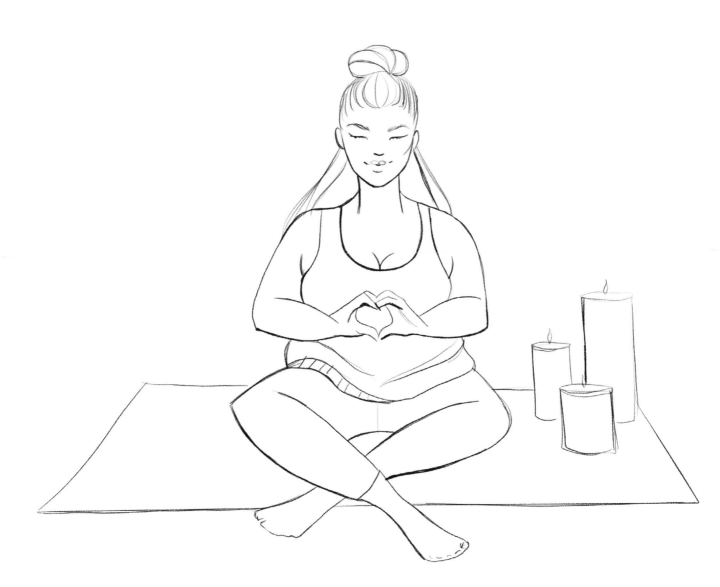

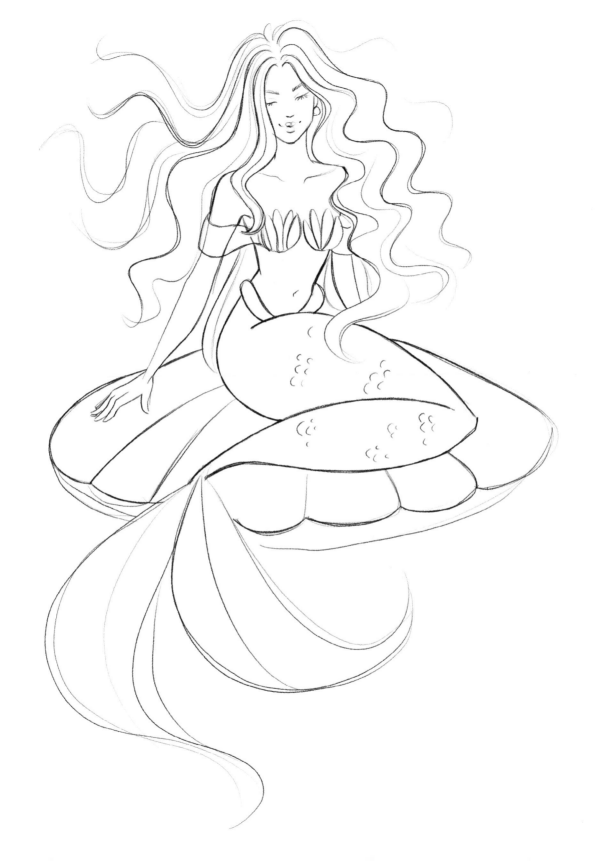

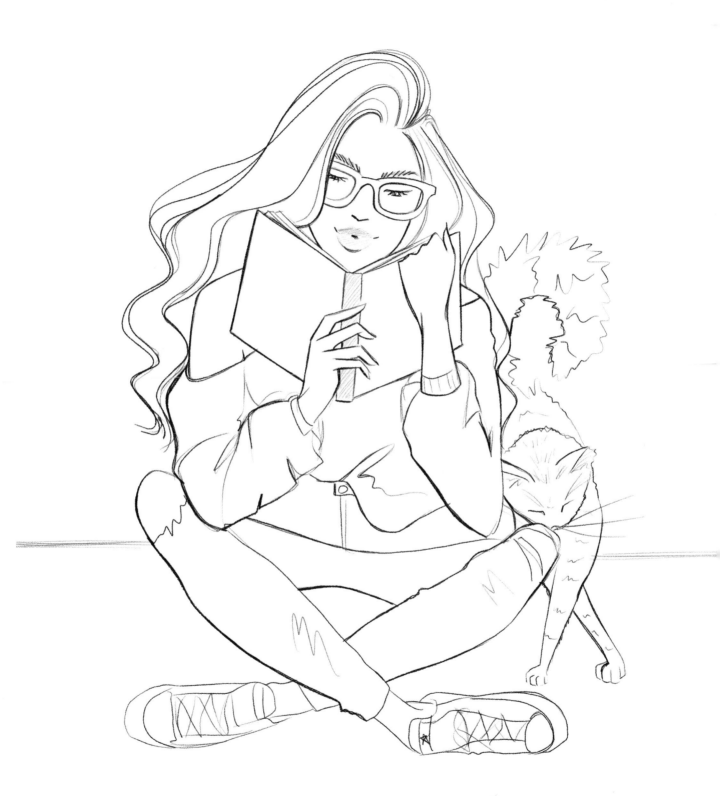

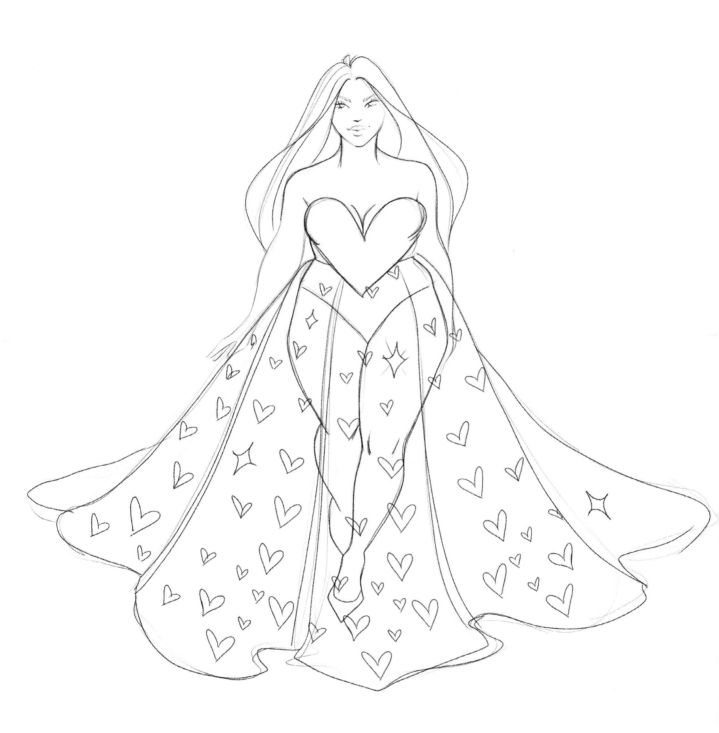

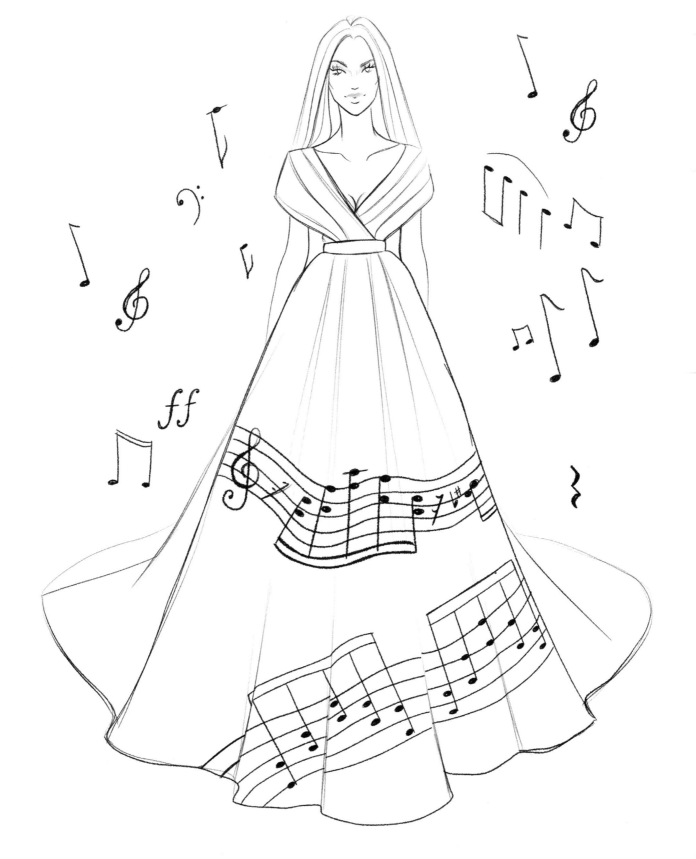

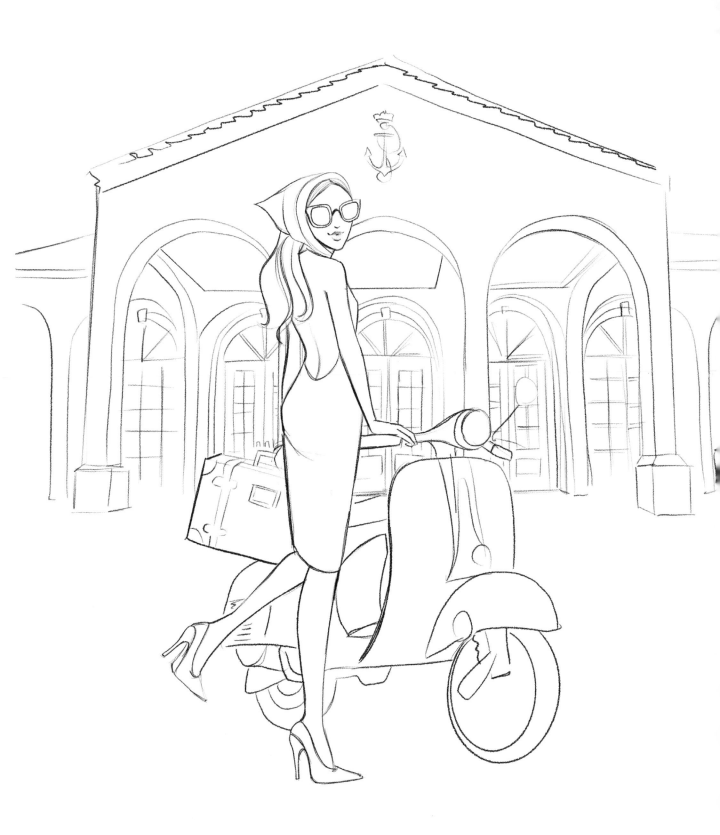

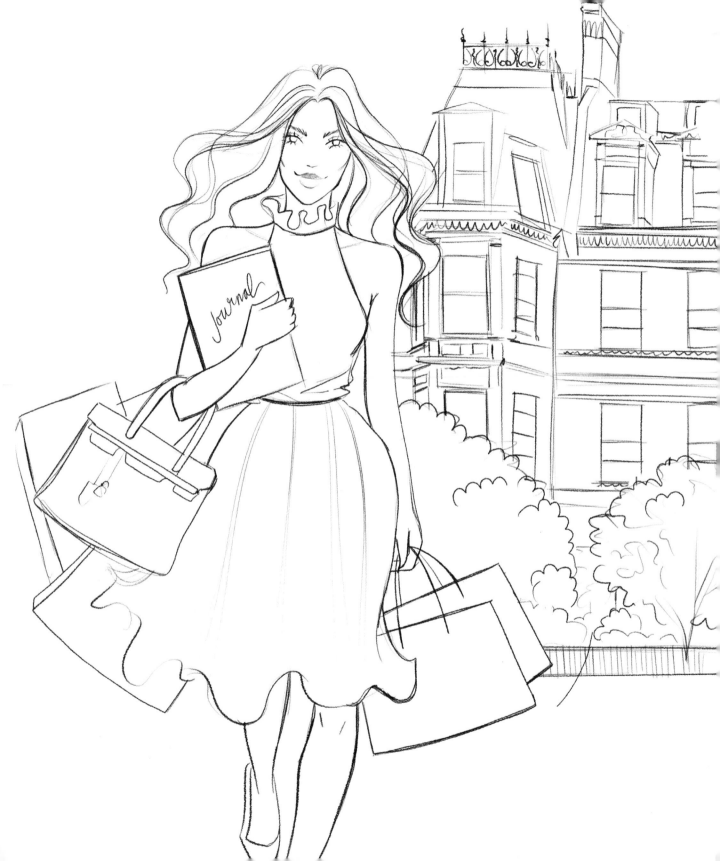

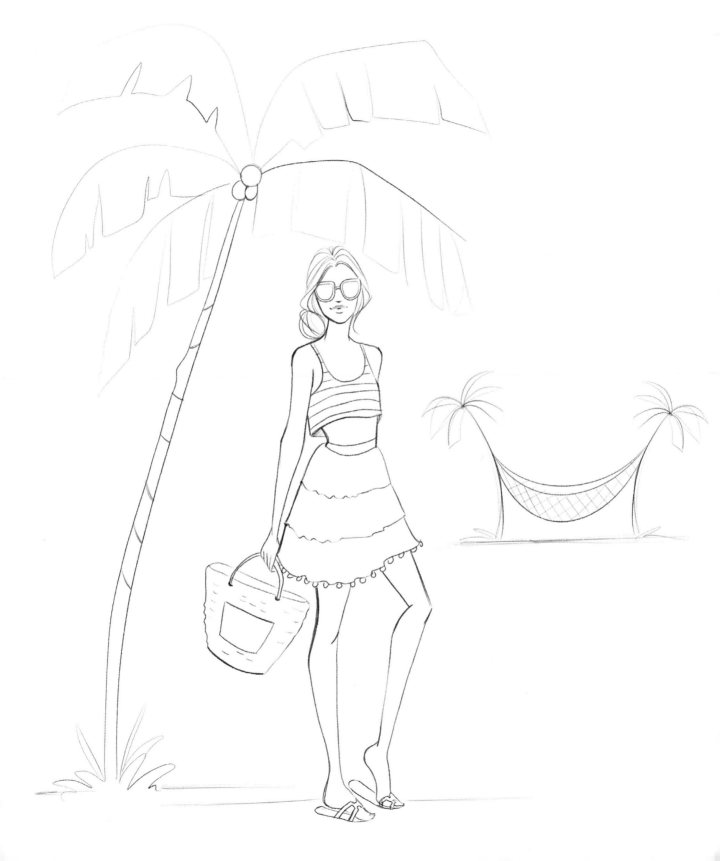

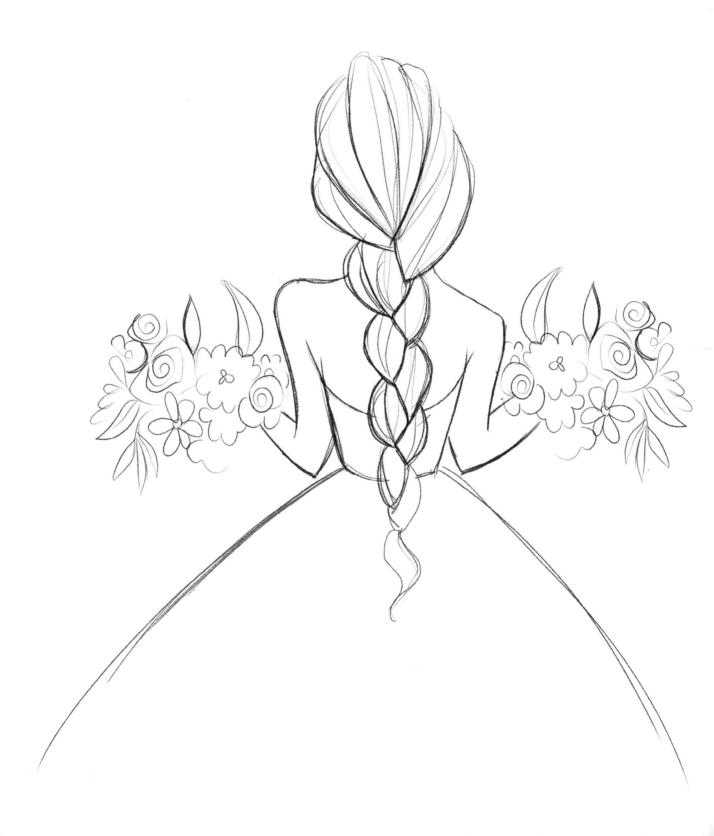

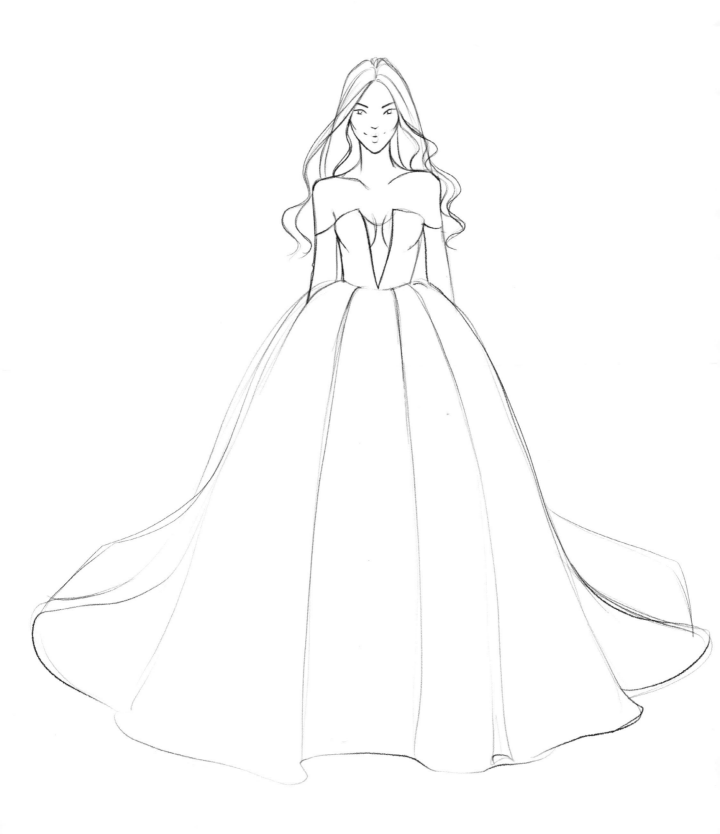

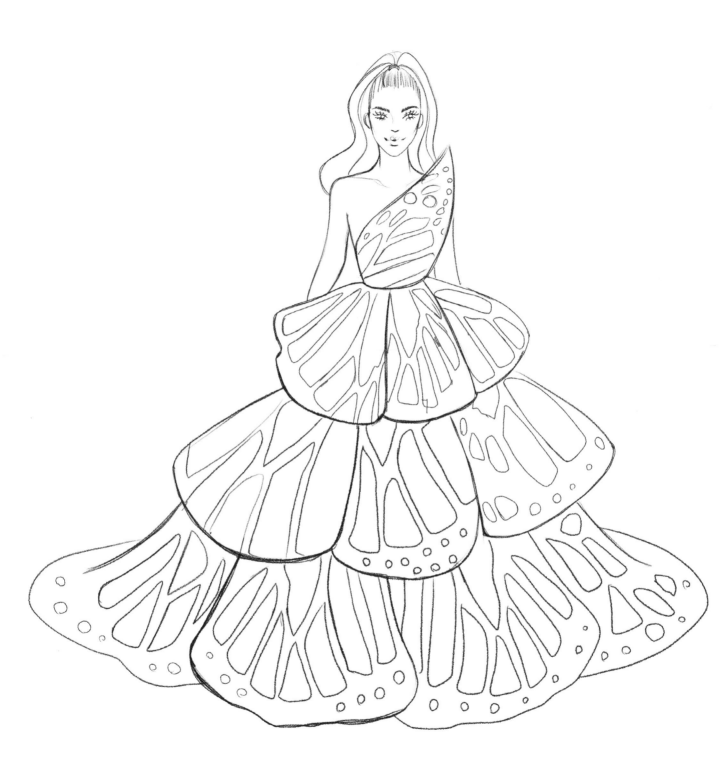

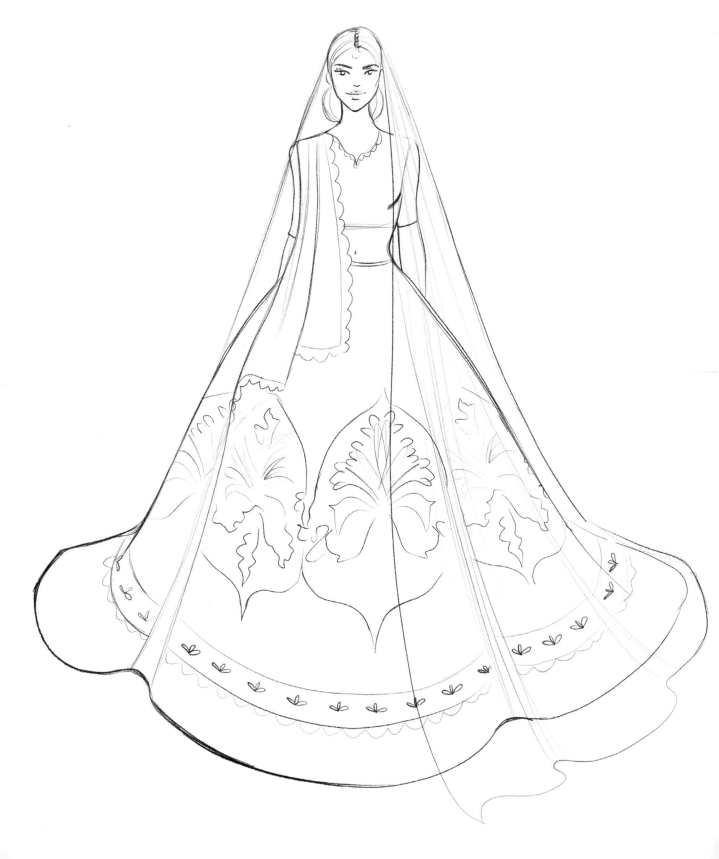

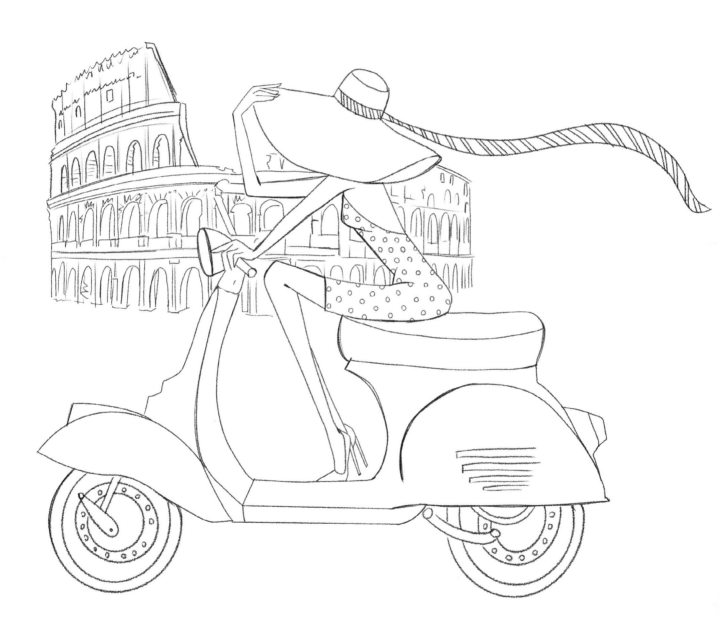

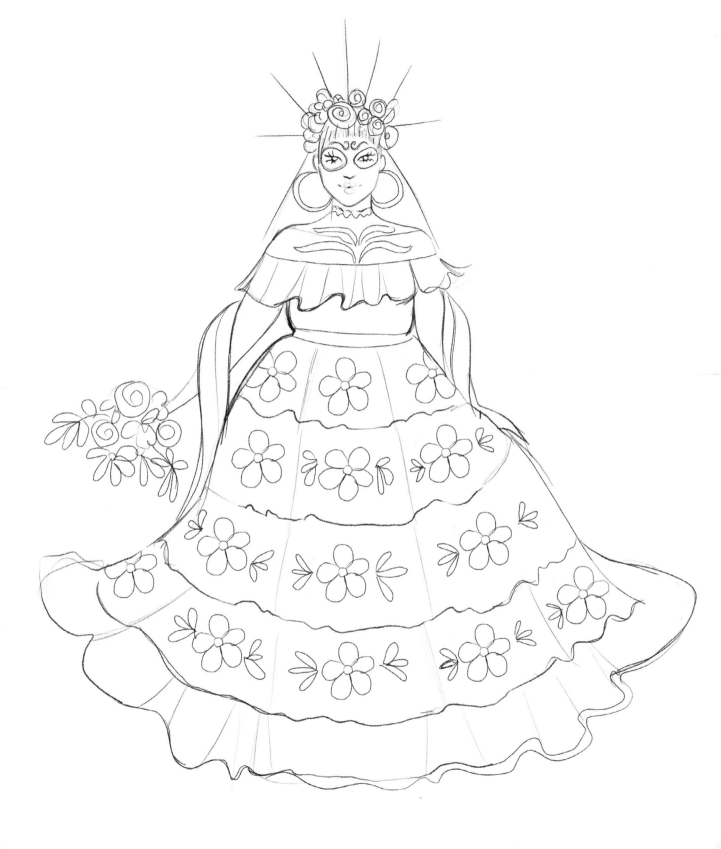

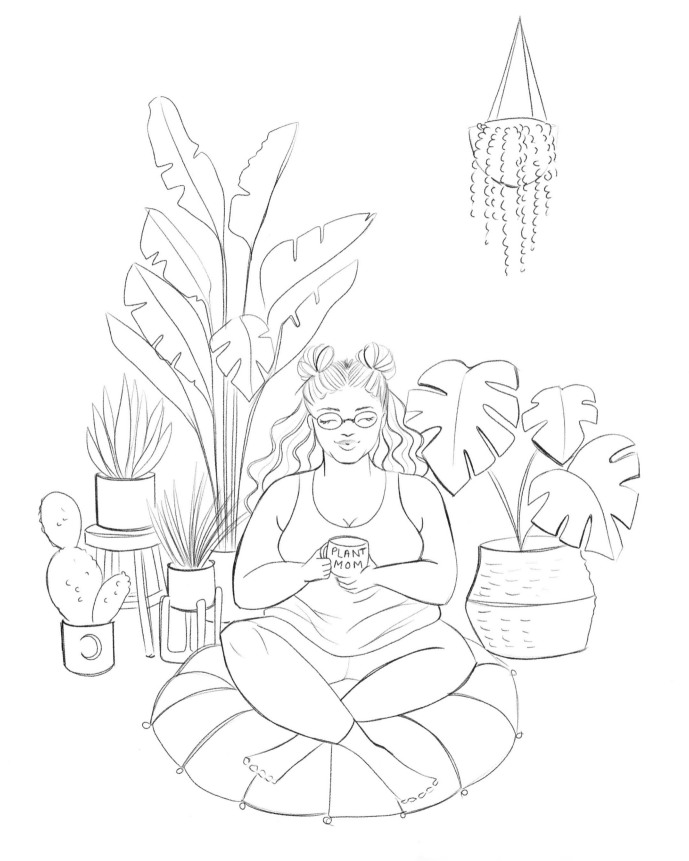

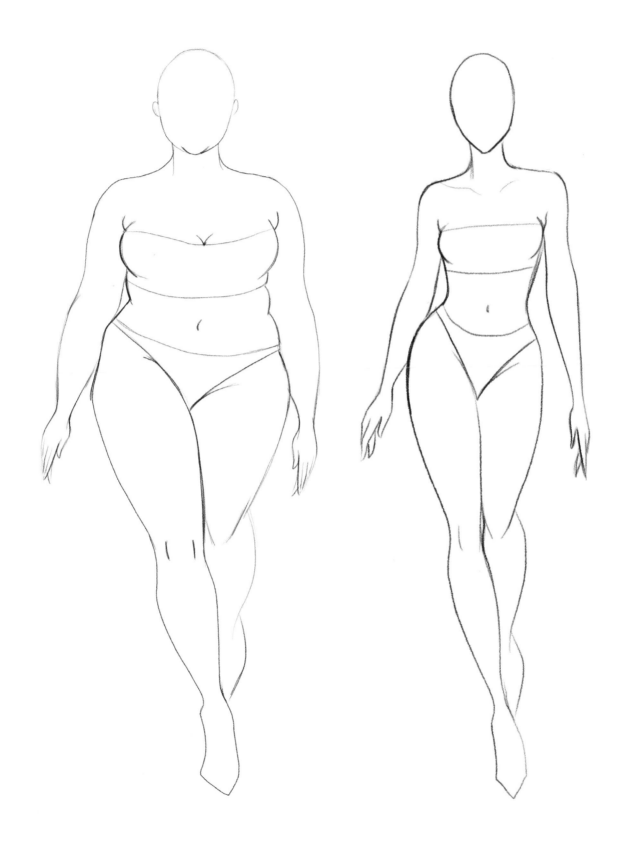

INSPIRATIONS

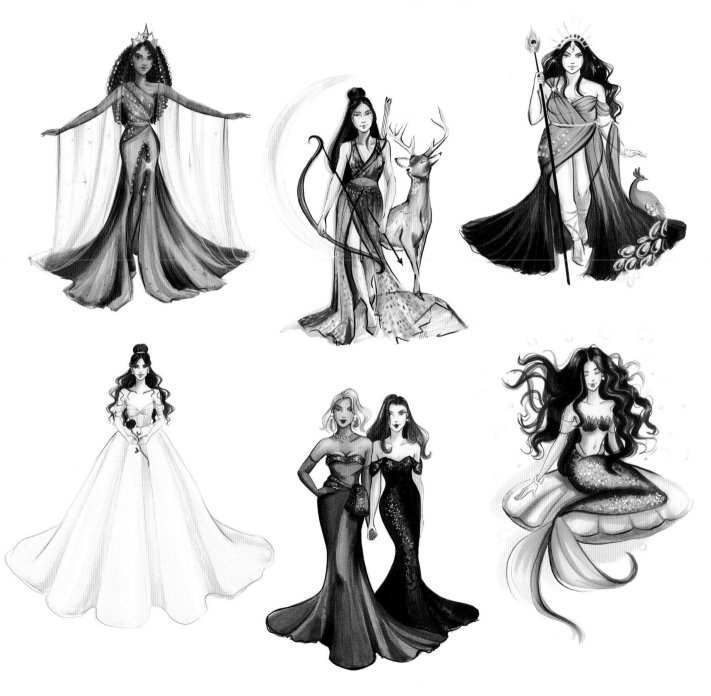

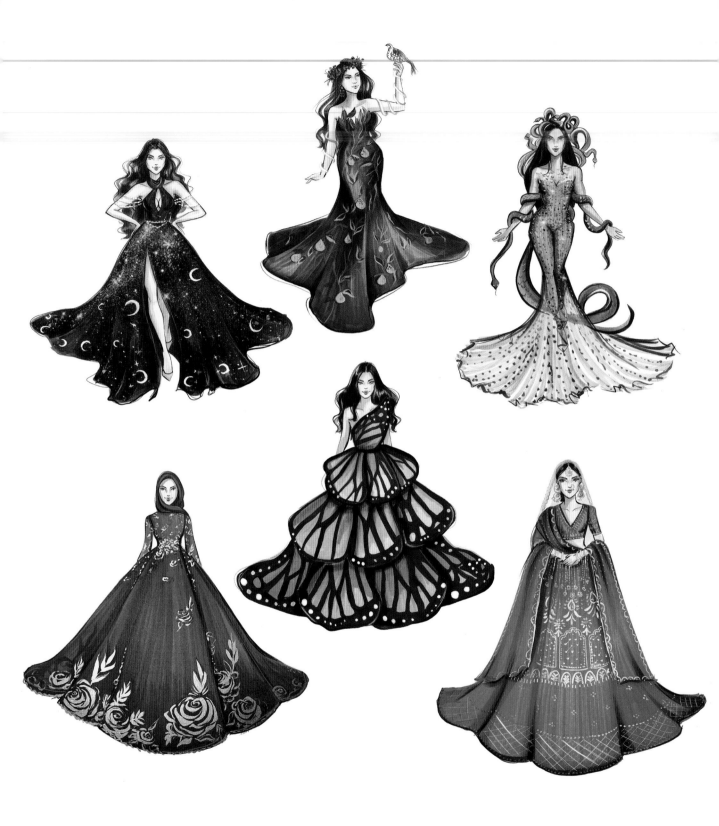

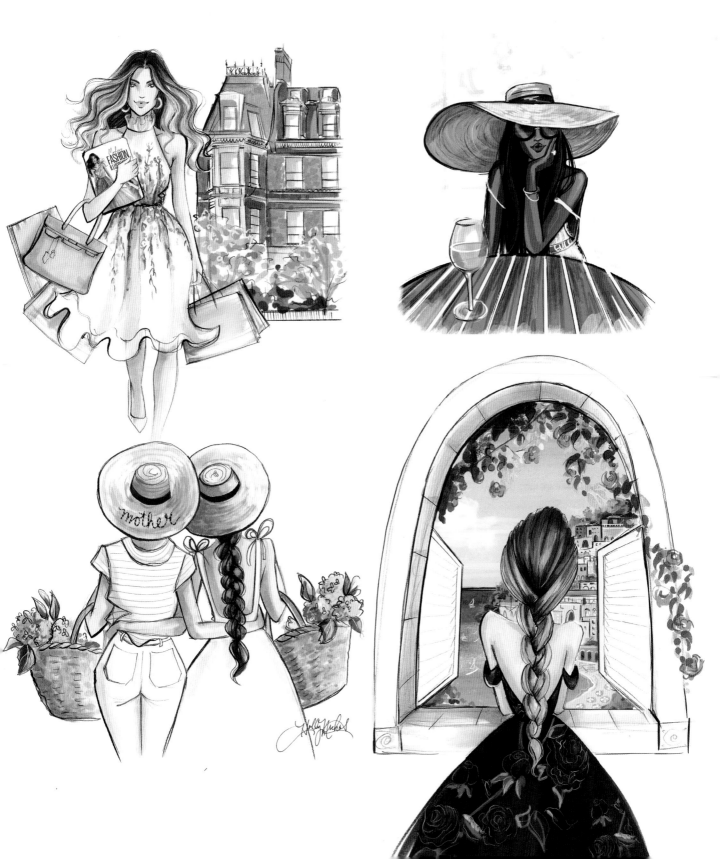

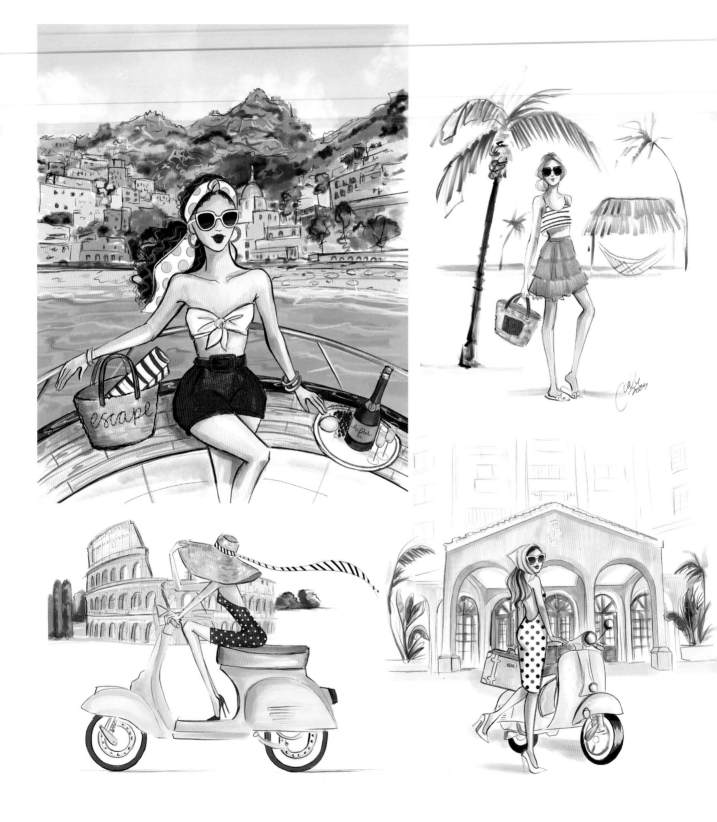

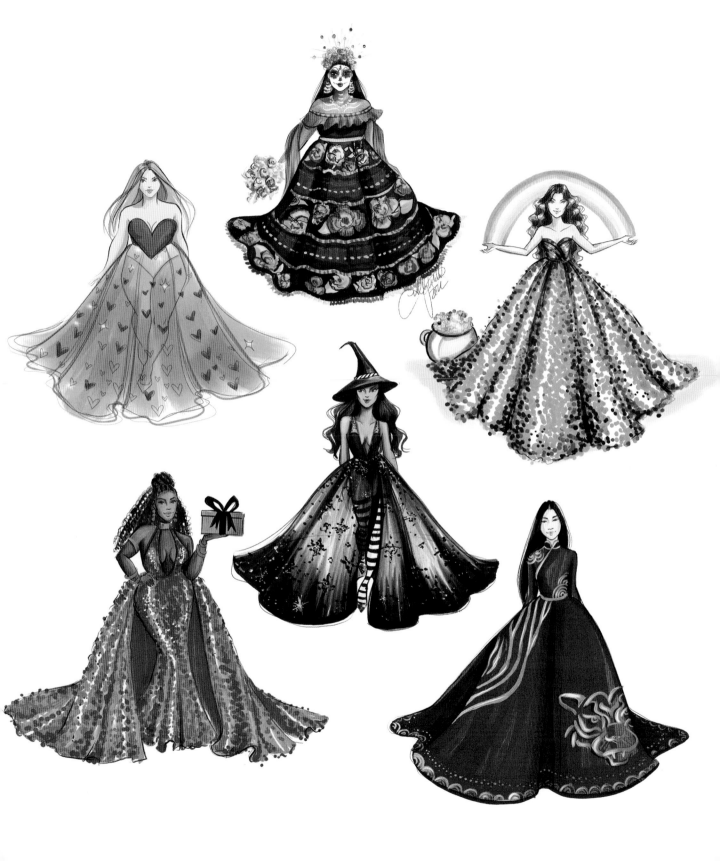

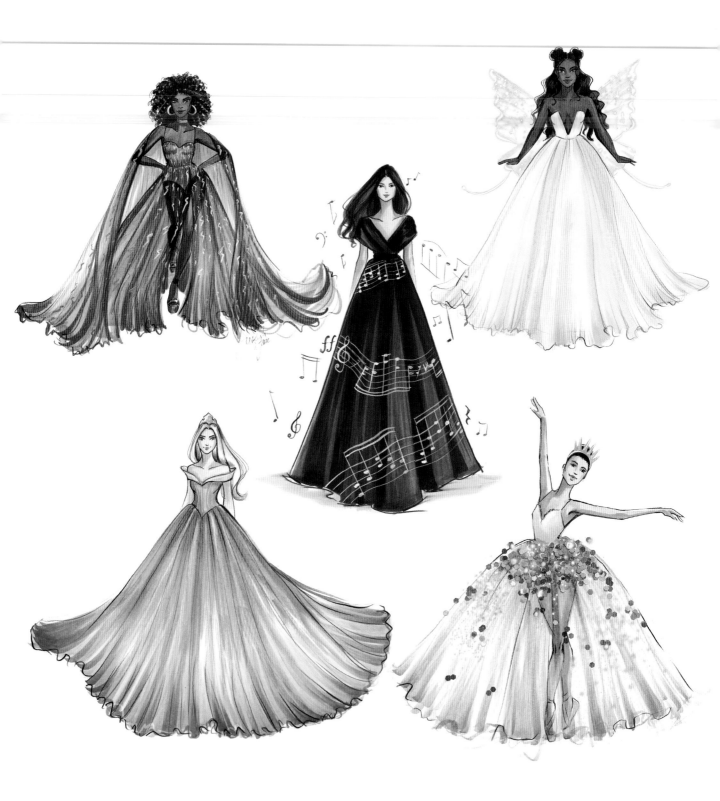

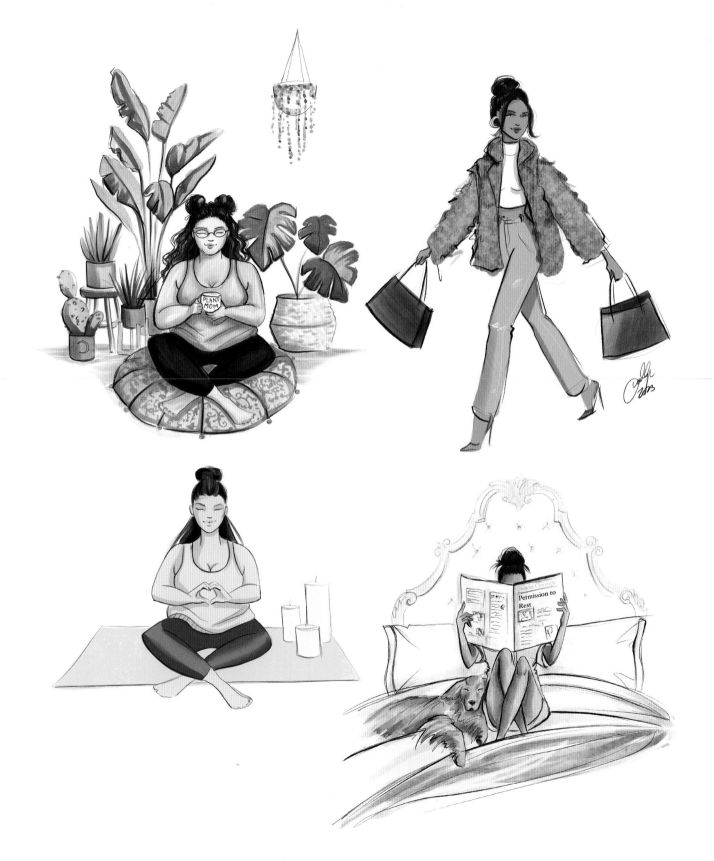

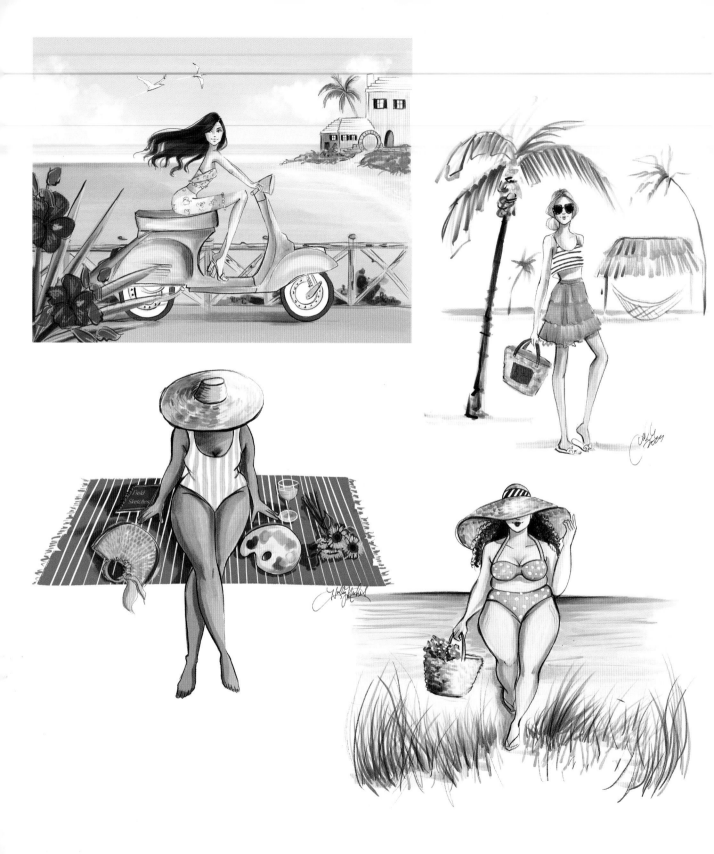